Sea Creatures
& other Favorite Animals

This library edition published in 2015 by Walter Foster Jr.,
an imprint of Quarto Publishing Group USA Inc.
6 Orchard Road, Suite 100
Lake Forest, CA 92630

Artwork © Fleurus Editions, Paris-2014
Published by Walter Foster Jr.,
an imprint of Quarto Publishing Group USA Inc.
Illustrated by Philippe Legendre
Written by Janessa Osle

Distributed in the United States and Canada by
Lerner Publisher Services
241 First Avenue North
Minneapolis, MN 55401 U.S.A.
www.lernerbooks.com

First Library Edition

Library of Congress Cataloging-in-Publication Data

Legendre, Philippe.
  Sea creatures & other favorite animals / by Philippe Legendre. -- First Library Edition.
     pages cm
  ISBN 978-1-939581-57-0
1. Animals in art--Juvenile literature. 2. Marine animals in art--Juvenile literature. 3. Drawing--Technique--Juvenile literature.
I. Legendre, Philippe, illustrator. II. Title. III. Title: Sea creatures and other favorite animals.
  NC780.O85 2015
  743.6--dc23

                                                                              2014026661

Printed in USA
9 8 7 6 5 4 3 2

Table of Contents

Tools & Materials

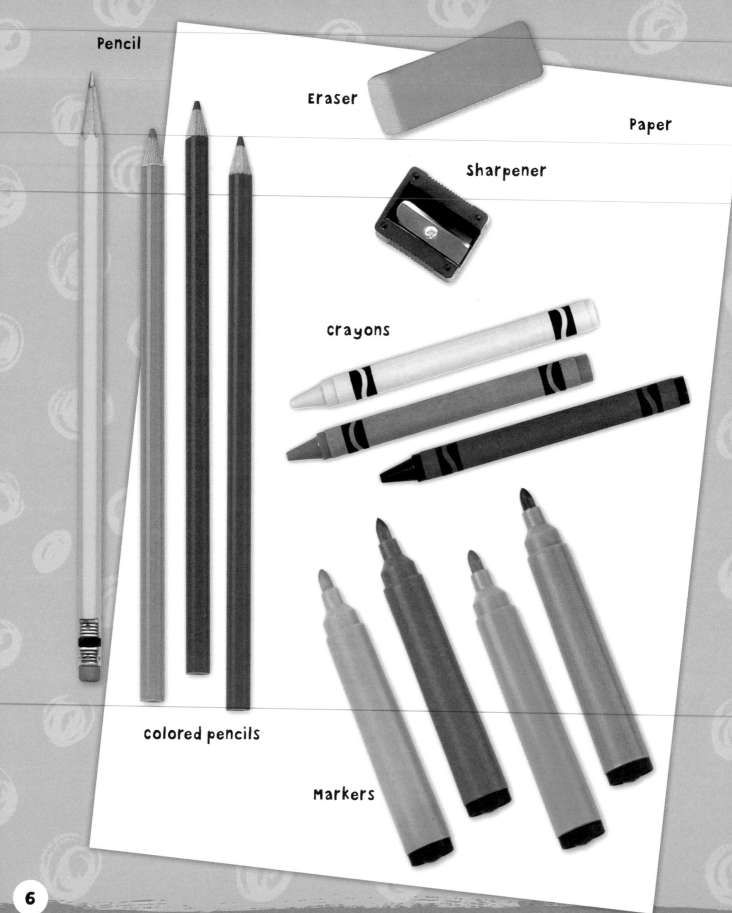

Pencil

Eraser

Paper

Sharpener

crayons

colored pencils

Markers

The Color Wheel

The color wheel shows the relationships between colors. It helps us understand how the different colors relate to and react with one another. It's easy to make your own color wheel!

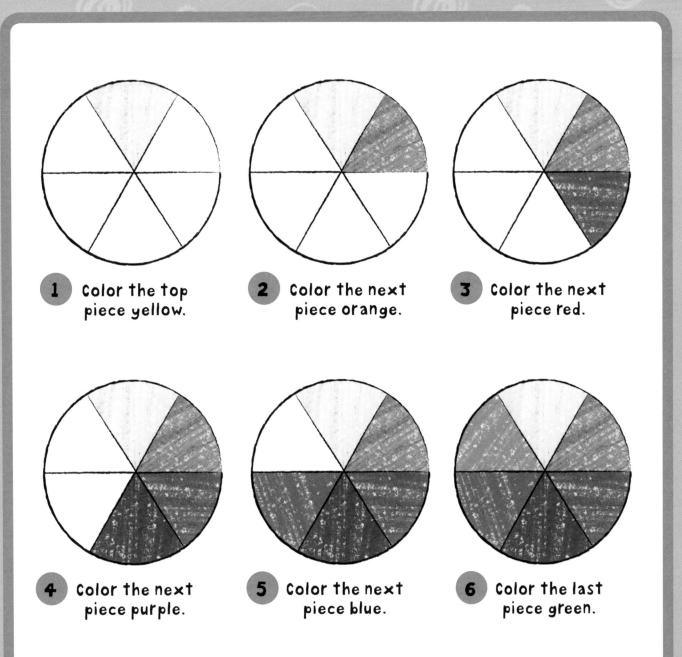

1 Color the top piece yellow.

2 Color the next piece orange.

3 Color the next piece red.

4 Color the next piece purple.

5 Color the next piece blue.

6 Color the last piece green.

Getting Started

Warm up your hand by drawing some squiggles and shapes on a piece of scrap paper.

Draw a square

Draw an oval

Draw a circle

Draw a rectangle

Draw a triangle

If you can draw a few basic shapes, you can draw just about anything!

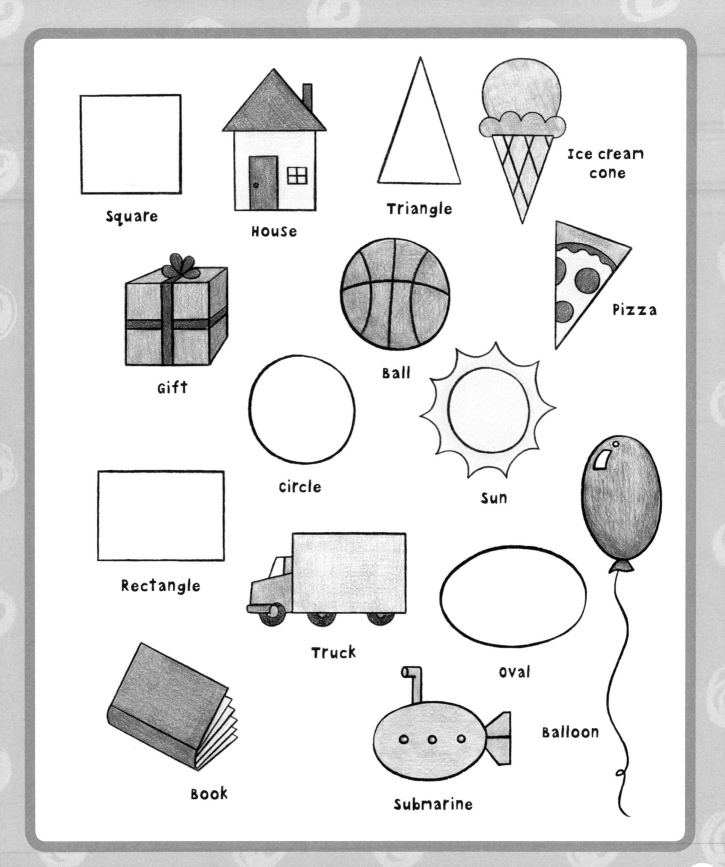

Square

House

Triangle

Ice cream cone

Gift

Ball

Pizza

circle

Sun

Rectangle

Truck

Oval

Balloon

Book

Submarine

starfish

If a starfish loses one of its arms, it can grow a new one!

Dolphin

Dolphins are very smart and playful animals.

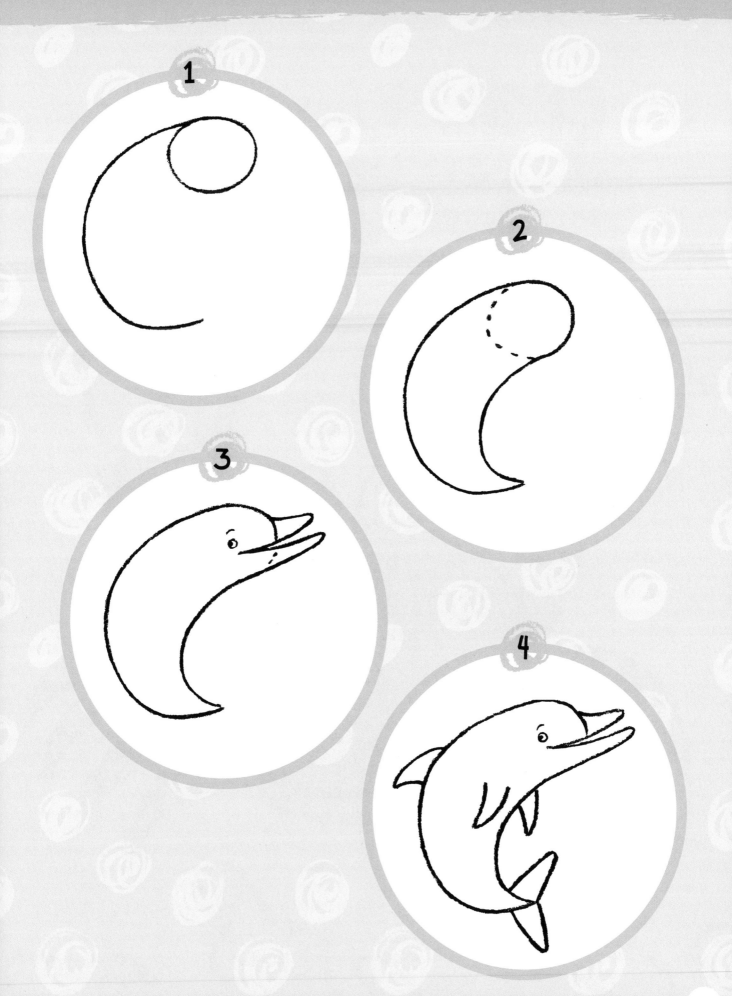

crab

This crustacean has a thick exoskeleton that protects it from predators.

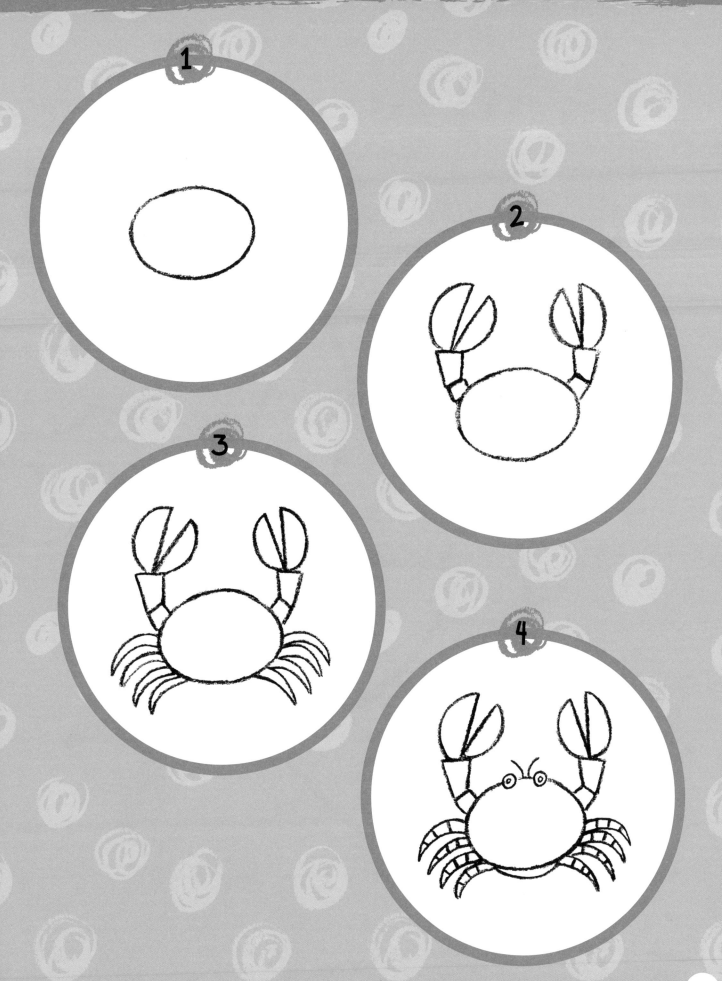

Seagull

This seabird can unhinge its jaw to eat large bites of food.

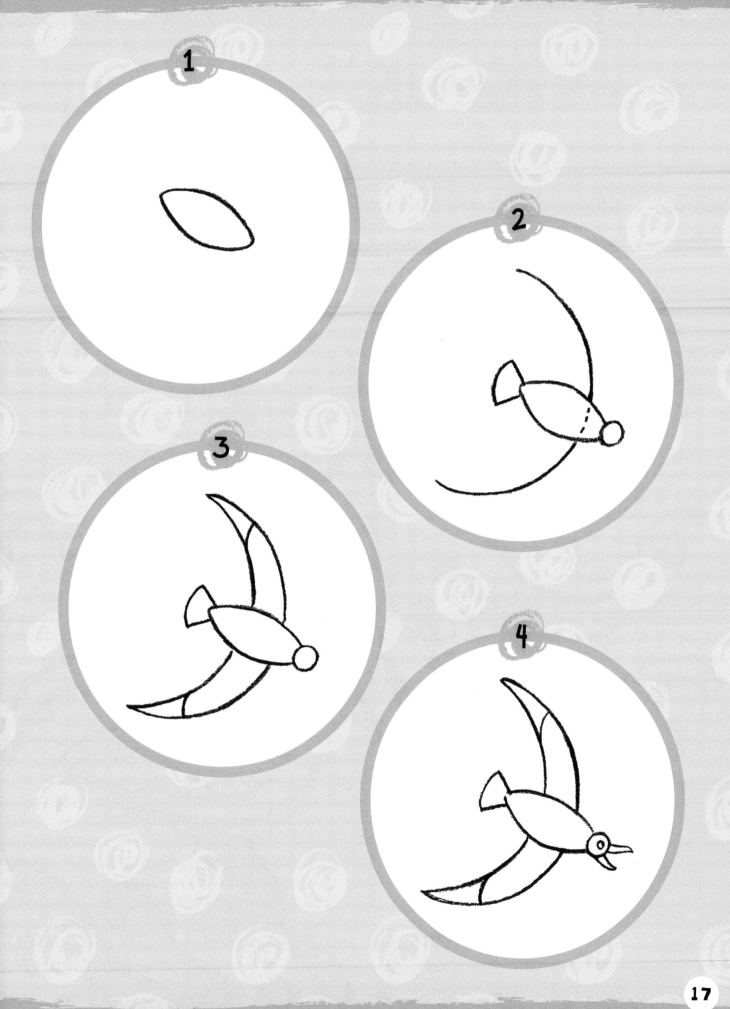

octopus

The octopus has eight arms that trail behind it as it swims.

Seashells

shells found on the beach once housed small creatures in the ocean.

Lamb

This little lamb is gentle and likes to graze all day long!

Baby Elephant

This baby elephant has a long trunk and likes to run alongside its mommy!

25

Kitten

This cute kitten likes to play with yarn!

Salmon

This large fish is born in freshwater, swims to the ocean, and then returns to freshwater as an adult.

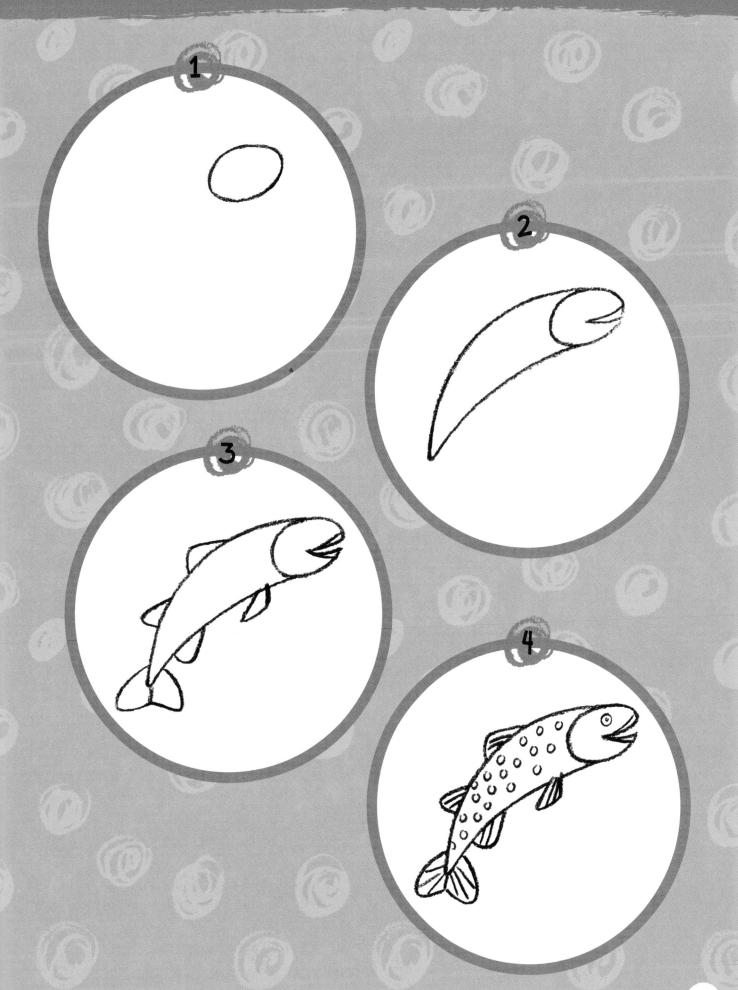

Mallard

This wild duck likes to swim around in ponds, marshes, lakes, and rivers.

Dragonfly

Dragonflies come in many different colors, including red, orange, green, and blue!

Kingfisher

This graceful bird dives into water to catch fish.

Heron

The heron has long legs and likes to wade in freshwater.

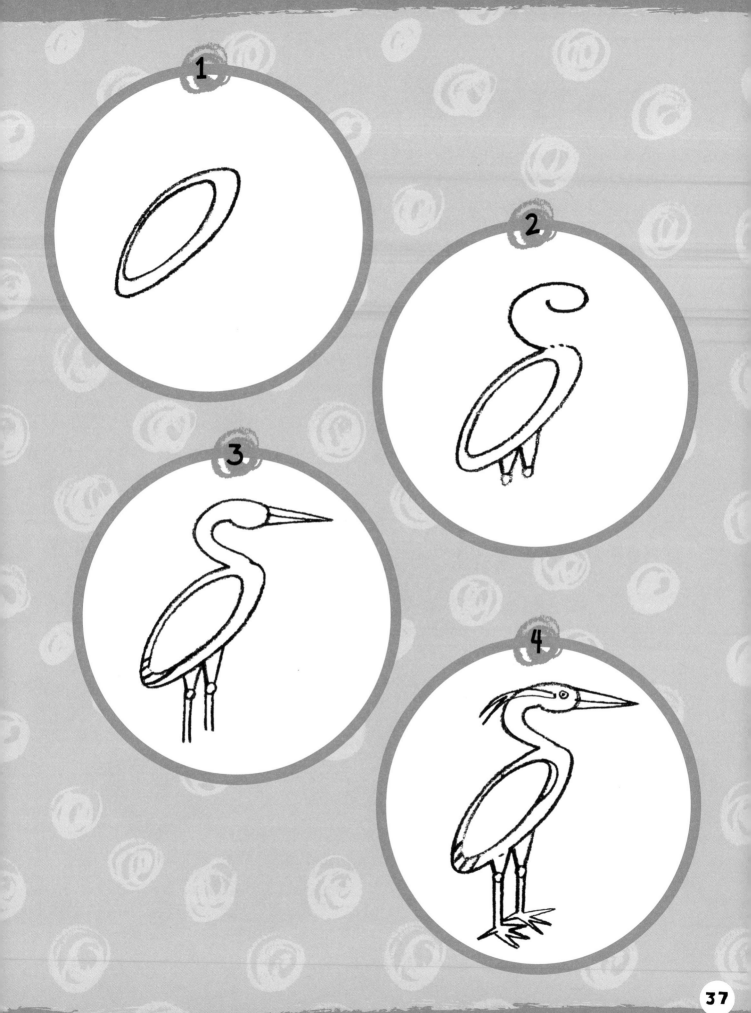

Beaver

Beavers build dams out of branches, stones, and mud to help make their homes.

Horse

Horses can sleep both standing up and lying down.

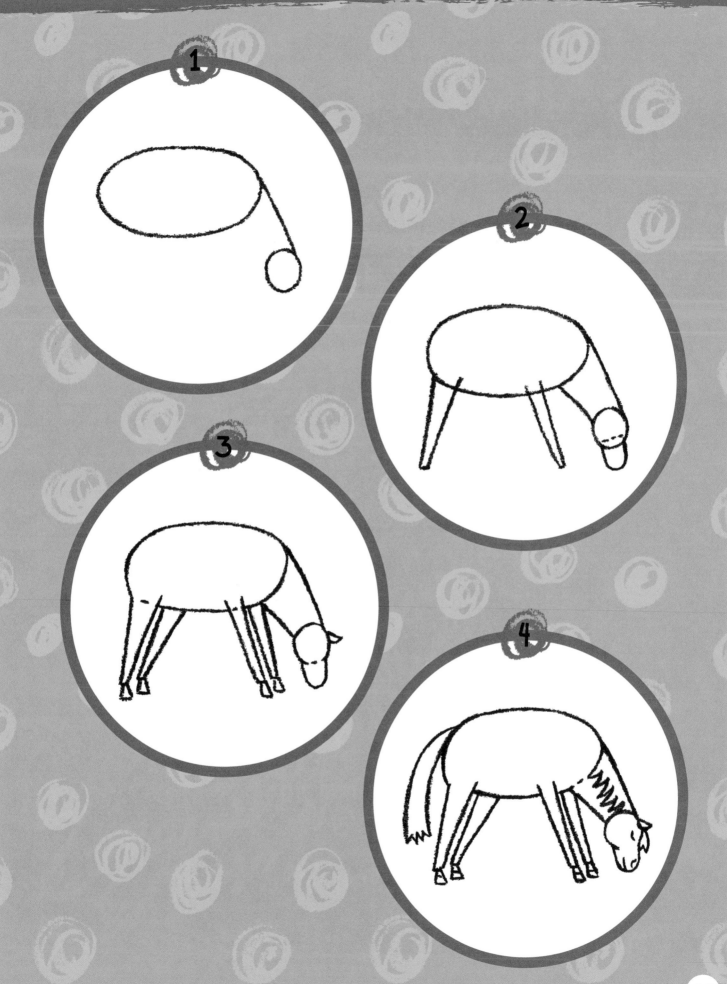

Cocker Spaniel

This dog has long floppy ears and a soft coat.

Owl

Most owls are nocturnal, meaning they are only active at night.

Frog

This amphibian has a long tongue and likes to sit on floating lily pads!

The End